G000055322

The Ramblings of the Man who Likes to Eat Alone

JAMES WEBB

CONTENTS

INTRODUCTION

The first year of my blog seemed to be well-received by about three people, and that is all it takes for me to feel the responsibility to keep going, so now you hold in your hands everything that I posted on my blog in its second year.

It's another year of thoughts, struggles, stories and celebrations – in short, it's another year of real life with God.

Sequels are generally a bit of a gamble. Rarely are they superior to the first release, but sometimes they manage to pull it off and then everyone talks about it for years. The handy thing about my blog, and these books, is that I have no idea whether they're any good or not. What I mean is that what I write is only any good if God uses it, and I have a limited control over that. This means that every time I write something, there's a chance that God will use it to be the best thing I have ever written for one particular person. That's exciting, and I forget it all the time. It also means that you never know when you might accidentally and unexpectedly read something that God uses to change your life.

But I'm making no promises. You might like this book, or you might not. You might think it's better than the last one, or you might not. That's fine. As long as about three people like it, I'll keep writing.

So whether through this book or not, may God bless you!

On Being Misunderstood

03 November 2016

*T*he *Second Listening Book* is now available from Amazon, and I thought that I should mention this in the blog. It's another collection of short stories and parables, ripe for misunderstanding. Being misunderstood is an occupational hazard for me. I've preached at least one sermon where my sophisticated and intelligent delivery (i.e. being too clever for my own good) was taken to mean that I was saying the *exact opposite* of what I was really trying to say, with hilarious consequences.

The meanings of the stories in *The Listening Book* and *The Second Listening Book* are sometimes clear and sometimes not. Although I had a very specific message in mind for each story as I wrote it, the purpose of the books is to create space for God, rather than me, to say something. Usually, what God wants to say is a lot more interesting than what I have to say. Still, if you're keen to try and discern what was in my head when I was writing, then there's plenty of scope for misunderstanding.

That's probably for the best though. Clarence Darrow, a lawyer, once said, "I have suffered from being misunderstood, but I would have suffered a lot more if I had been understood." I wonder if that might be true for me too. After all, calling others to rethink their way of looking at the world can get you into a lot of trouble. When Jesus was misunderstood they scratched their heads, said "What is he talking about?" and thought that he was mad, but when they began to understand, they wanted him dead.

Do Motives Matter?

10 November 2016

I've recently been thinking about Ruth's motives. No, not my Ruth – the Old Testament Ruth. What was it that motivated her to commit to her mother-in-law, leave her country and start all over again in a strange land? The conclusion that I came to is that perhaps it doesn't matter what her motives were. The important thing was that she put herself at God's mercy – why she did it might not be important.

I remember the early days of each year at Canowindra, seeing a row of new first-year students, grinning like the little sunbeams that they were. "Why have you come to Cornerstone?" we'd ask. "Because we want to grow and be more like Jesus!" they'd say. As the months rolled on, and the real motives began to surface, you'd realise that some of them should have just pleaded the Fifth Amendment.

But it was the same for them as it was for Ruth. They'd left family, friends and the familiar for the unknown hardships of rural central west Australia. The fact that they'd come was more important than why they'd come. They'd foolishly put themselves in a place where God could get at them, and He just got on with the business of transforming lives, regardless of motives.

With suspiciously good timing, I found myself reading Paul's letter to the Philippians during these reflections. In that letter Paul identifies two groups of preachers – the ones who used Christ as a means of stirring up trouble for the Church, and the ones who did it for love of God. "But who cares," says Paul, "as long as Christ is being proclaimed?" God will always be building His kingdom, it's just that sometimes He uses the devil to do it.

I'm not saying that motives don't matter. Sometimes they matter a lot; sometimes they're the only thing that matters, and everything done out of wrong motives will be burnt away and none of those nice-looking deeds will be left standing. I'm just saying that sometimes motives don't matter. God can judge our motives, and God decides when those motives matter.

Fishers of Men?

17 November 2016

I'm beginning to come round to the idea that there's no such thing as a shallow person. I think that we all have depth; we all have significant, meaningful needs. What we think of as a 'shallow person' is just someone who hasn't realised just how deep their identity goes, and tries to meet profound needs with shallow, disposable things. Comfort Eating, Retail Therapy and Binge Watching all work, but not for long.

When Jesus is walking by the Sea of Galilee and meets Simon and Andrew he tells them that if they come with him, he will make them 'fishers of men'. It's a strange offer, but I believe that it connected with something deep in the two men. Maybe it harmonised with something they didn't even know about themselves? It must have done something powerful – "At once they left their nets and followed him."

Maybe Simon and Andrew wanted more than just fishing? Perhaps they wanted to make their lives count for something more than the marketplace?

That's what Jesus offered them, and I believe that – if we'll listen – he makes a similar call to each of us, something unique that meets a deep hunger within our souls.

That encounter on the banks of the Sea of Galilee was once suggested to me as a mediation. Spend some time in silence, calming your heart and mind. Then picture the seashore, the waves flapping nearby, the sound and smells of the breeze, the hustle and bustle of fishermen coming and going, engaging in their life's work. Imagine that you are there, just minding your own business, and then suddenly you look up. Jesus is standing there. He looks at you and says, "Come, follow me, and I will…"

Well? What does he say? How does he finish that sentence? "Come, follow me, and I will…" What is it that he offers you that resonates with your soul, makes your heart burn within you and gives you no choice but to walk away from your nets?

A Metaphor

24 November 2016

There was once a boy who wanted to make a difference. He worked hard at this, but was often left frustrated by how little change he saw. On one particularly frustrating day, he took a scrap of paper, wrote on it TRUST IN JESUS, rolled it up and put it in an empty glass bottle. Then he took that bottle down to the beach and threw it into the sea as hard as he could. It didn't really make him feel any better, but at least, he thought, he was doing something.

The bottle bobbed by the shore for a while, before it was carried out into the big, wide ocean. It drifted for many days and nights, around shoals of fish, reefs, deserted islands and one very surprised shark whose life may have taken a radically new direction if he had learned to read. Eventually the bottle washed ashore on a beach in a different place in a different country.

That evening, a man was walking in the surf, bare-foot and reflective. He was meditating on the meaning of life just as the bottle bumped against the side of his foot. He bent down, picked it up and opened it. He pulled out the note and read it: TRUST IN JESUS. Because the man had been thinking, and had already taken his shoes off, he was changed.

Meanwhile, in a different place in a different country, the boy was still pacing up and down, frustrated because he wasn't making a difference.

Fair Trade

01 December 2016

This is an edited version of a sermon I once preached (though I've not edited it much). It's a true account, though the lesson I was taught took a while to formulate and wasn't delivered to me in the divine monologue that I have written here. However, I knew that when I told this story I wanted to present it as something personal that took place between God and myself, because it was...

I used to play a lot of video games. I would fund this hobby by selling games when I was done with them, and using the money to buy new games. Once I was selling quite a few games on eBay and I had plans for the money. I wanted to get this one particular game – a rare and (relatively) expensive game.

That was my plan anyway.

On the day that the eBay auctions were due to end, I was in a good mood. It looked like I was going to end up with enough money to buy not only the game that I wanted, but another rare and (relatively) expensive game that I also had my eye on.

That morning, I was praying.

"Your eBay auctions are doing well, aren't they James?" said God, out of nowhere.

"Oh no, God. I'm not going to talk to you about those auctions. Let's talk about something else. How about the weather? It's a nice day, isn't it? Good job on that, by the way," I said.

God ploughed on. "I've got an idea. Why don't you give away all the money that you make from the auctions?"

"I knew it!" I said. "This is why I don't talk to you about this kind of thing! I knew you were going to say that!"

"Well aren't you the clever one. So what about it? I think you'll learn something from it."

All day I wrestled with this, but I knew there was only going to be one outcome.

"OK. You win, God," I said.

That evening the auctions ended, and they ended with me making enough money to buy at least two and a half rare and (relatively) expensive games. There I was with this money, which was God's, and all these games that I had to ship off to people who had no idea how miserable they had made me.

God must have noticed that I wasn't my usual bubbly self.

"Something wrong, James?"

"You know what's wrong, God."

"What's the problem? It wasn't as if it was a huge sum of money, was it?"

"It's not the amount, God. It's what it was for. I really wanted that game. I know it's silly. I know it's only a little thing, but it mattered to me. If you'd asked me to just give, even double that amount, I would have done it without even thinking twice, but that particular money was mine. I had plans for it."

"Ah. I think we're getting somewhere," said God. "You know, Jesus pointed that out to his disciples. Do you remember the widow who gave her penny to the Temple? Compared to the many who were dumping wealth into the Temple treasury her gift was nothing, but Jesus knew that it was something, because to give that meant that she had to go without. In other words, it meant something to Jesus because it cost her something *here*. And a long time before that, David, my servant knew this too.

"The land of Israel had wandered from me, and David had been a part of this. I brought my punishment on the people, and David recognised that it was his fault, his responsibility. So he said 'God, let me make reparation,' and went to make a sacrifice to appease me. Araunah offered him a piece of land to build an altar, to worship me. But David said 'No,' because David knew. David knew that it wasn't about the altar, it wasn't about the worship, and David knew that – as the king, as the guilty party – the cost had to be his. He couldn't make appeasement from what was left over after he had his fill. It had to mean something to him. It had to cost him something *here*. You know what he said, James? He said 'I will not offer to the Lord my God burnt offerings that have cost me nothing.' He was saying, 'I will not bring to my God worship that isn't a sacrifice.'

"You see, the sacrifice is not measured in its size or how elaborate it is. The sacrifice is measured in what it costs you *here*. You're right. It hurt you to give that particular gift. For many people what I asked you to do wouldn't be a sacrifice, so I wouldn't ask them to do it. I asked you because I knew that it would cost you something, truly, where it mattered. Right *here*. I knew that you would be giving something that you didn't want to give. I knew that you couldn't just do it on automatic pilot and throw out a gesture – you needed to make a conscious decision to put me first. That's the measure of a sacrifice. I know that what it would hurt one person to give would be no big deal for another. If it's not a big deal, then it's not a sacrifice. If it doesn't hurt you to give a million pounds, then it's not a sacrifice. If it doesn't hurt you to give up a holiday, then it's not a sacrifice. If it doesn't hurt you to follow me, then it's not a sacrifice. If it doesn't cost you something *here* then it's not a sacrifice. And if it's not a sacrifice, why should I see any merit in it? Do you think I'm a bird and that you can feed me with the crumbs of what you have left over? Why should I consider it a gift?

"You know, you can't ever judge the sacrifice of another human being without knowing what it's cost them *here*. You can be judgemental, but you can't judge. You can look at something and say 'That's no big deal,' but only I know whether it's a big deal and therefore only I know the sacrifice. And I know that it cost you to give me that small sum of money. I know that it really cost you to go without a toy that would hold absolutely no interest to the vast majority of sane, rational people. I know this, and that's why it was a sacrifice and that's why it pleased me. That's why *you* pleased me. David knew this. David knew it in his heart – and now you know it. This is what you're getting in return for that money. Not a game, not even two or three games, but this knowledge. Fair trade?"

"Yes God," I said. "Fair trade. Thank you."

Another Guest Post from Rev. Ulysses Giblet

08 December 2016

All right. The Rev. Ulysses Giblet has been e-mailing me every week for the past three months asking when I'm was going to let him '…share his great gift with the world' again, so for the sake of peace and quiet here he is. Enjoy, or whatever.

James has been begging me to write another guest post, so here it is. Today I will be writing about prayer and the role it has to play in public worship.

There are few aspects of public worship as versatile as prayer. Prayer can be used to fill an awkward silence, to give the musicians time to get back into position, to communicate important news to the congregation ("Lord, we pray for the REALLY IMPORTANT SERVICE that we're having next Thursday, at 7pm, parking is limited so don't be late.") and much more! What else can you use to get the whole congregation to close their eyes for a moment while you deal with an embarrassing itch? Being skilled in the art of prayer is crucial for anyone who is involved in leading a church service. Luckily for you, I'm here to offer some gold-plated advice and get you up to speed.

Here are my top tips for public prayer:

1. DO use as many long words as possible. The fewer people that understand your prayer, the more impressed God is.

2. DON'T forget to throw in a few 'Words From The Lord' every now and then. It's very easy to do, and keeps the rubes – I mean, congregation - on their toes. Something like "What's that, Lord? Someone here is struggling with trusting God? We pray for that brother and/or sister." You can keep it vague, and you're bound to be 100% accurate, or you can be as specific and detailed as you like – who's going to know if you're wrong?

3. DO use a special voice. Do you really think God is impressed with whatever regional dialect you normally communicate in? Do you think God listens to, or even understands, what you're saying in your Irish brogue, Texan drawl, or - heaven forbid - Scouse whine? No.

Remember, God loves you best when you sound like a BBC newsreader from the 1960s.

4. DON'T make your prayers too short. The longer you pray, the better your prayer and - consequently - the better Christian you are. Also, the more time it gives you to deal with that awkward itch. Some people may tell you that Jesus said something about the length of your prayers not mattering, but it's clear to even the most simple-minded scholar that those verses have been taken out of context, just like all those other verses that people use to contradict me.

5. DO use prayer time to let the congregation know about your new book releases and other revenue streams. "Lord, I just want to take this moment to thank you for the release of my new book - *Preach and Pray the Giblet Way* - which is available at the back of the church at the very reasonable price of £9.99. Signed copies extra." Again, some naive people might say that prayer should really be about God, but let's face it, it's not as if He needs the money.

If you remember these five simple tips you'll be well on your way to earning your Public Prayer Badge and soaking up some of the respect and adoration that you're due. You're welcome.

We Don't Believe in Jesus Anymore. We Believe in Colouring-in

15 December 2016

The title of this post is a line that I've had floating around in my head for a couple of weeks. It feels like it wants to be the punchline to a poem, but that sounds like too much hard work at the moment.

What does the line mean? It's my response to the whole 'mindfulness' craze. Mindfulness is about trying to enjoy and focus on the present moment, and acknowledging your current emotions while not letting them control you. I'm not actually opposed to that. I think that being 'mindful' is a good thing, as attempts to live deliberately often are. Actually, between you and me, I think that it's a spiritual discipline, with a fine tradition in Christian spirituality, and that's where my problem lies.

It's like people have finally realised that there's something deeply wrong with the country's soul, and have correctly identified that a big part of the problem is the poverty of the average Westerner's inner life. Man shall not live on bread alone, and all that. But the problem is that we can't acknowledge that religion might have something to contribute to this discussion, so we try mindfulness. It works for our society because you don't have to believe in anything to be mindful. You can even offer it in schools without offending anyone – and that's the most important thing about education, after all.

So now, the solution to the stress and alienation of twenty-first century living is to go down to *The Works* and buy yourself a mindfulness colouring-in book. As Roy Walker, of *Catchphrase*, used to say – "It's good, but it's not right!"

I have read in Plato and Cicero sayings that are very wise and very beautiful; but I have never read in either of them: "Come to me, all you who are weary and burdened, and I will give you rest."

St. Augustine

Looking Forward to Christmas

22 December 2016

I like the build up to Christmas. I like the festive lights, nostalgic songs and the general atmosphere. I even enjoy the weather – the crisp, cold winter days. In Australia we had nine months of summer and three months of grim misery in a house that was designed to shed as much heat as possible. Plus, Christmas in the summer just felt wrong.

Christmas day itself is usually an anti-climax, with all kinds of pitfalls that need negotiating – such as having to go to church when *it's not even a Sunday*. No, I think I like pre-Christmas better. Stress and family drama aside, people seem a bit happier in the build up to Christmas. It's almost as if, for a moment, faith and hope have become part of the public life. As people begin to actually look forward to something special, there's a kind of universal mini-expression of the Gospel happening, even without reference to the Christmas story. One of the greatest gifts of God through Christ is, I think, hope.

C.S. Lewis put it masterfully when he described Narnia under the White Witch as a place where it's always winter but never Christmas. Just as the hope of Christmas changes the nation for a short while, so the hope of the message of Christ can give us a foundation of hope for our whole lives. People just seem to do better when they have hope – it's almost as if there's something in our DNA that was made for faith. Without hope, life is just hard work.

Some of you many know the story of Alexander Solzhenitsyn, the Russian author. He was sentenced to eight years hard labour in a Soviet gulag for making 'disrespectful' remarks about Stalin in a private letter to a friend. His time in the gulag broke him, and one day he just walked away from his work team and sat down on the ground. He had given up and wanted to die, and this was his way of provoking the guards into killing him. An old man moved apart from his own group and sat down beside Solzhenitsyn. The old man picked up a stick and drew a crude outline of a cross in the sand, and then got up and walked back to his work team. As Solzhenitsyn looked at that cross he realised that hope was always possible for the followers of Jesus, indeed, in a place like this, it was the only hope one could have. Solzhenitsyn didn't die that day. He survived the camp and, after his release, became one of the most celebrated Russian authors of all time, writing about faith and freedom.

That story seems like a bit of a downer. It's not very Christmasy, is it? But, as I think about hope and faith and a Christmas that lasts beyond crisp winters, mince pies and Slade, maybe it is quite a Christmasy story after all.

Musings on Faith, Reason, Experience, Colouring-in and Worship

29 December 2016

It's been one of those years – the kind of year that was meant by the ancient Chinese curse, "May you live in Interesting Times."

Here's a couple of things I find interesting about these Interesting Times. The first is that, through following up on Tweets and stuff, I learned that in America three of the top five best-selling non-fiction Christian books of 2016 were adult colouring-in books. After what I wrote a couple of weeks ago, I don't know what to say. I understand that some people find them helpful, but really? *Three out of five?*

I also learnt, through following links on my friend Terry's blog, that Chris Tomlinson's song 'Good, Good Father' won the GMA Dove Song of the year at the Dove Awards. The author of the piece that I read offers a substantial critical assessment of the song. The most intriguing point that he makes is that there's nothing exclusively Christian about the song other than the use of the name 'Father' to refer to God. I find it interesting that the 'Christian Song of the Year' doesn't mention Jesus, or anything explicitly Christian at all. Again, I've commented before on worship, but I find this...interesting.

So, what do these two things mean, if anything? Is it just coincidental noise, or do they hint at something about Western Christianity? Are they a symptom of the dreaded 'dumbing down' that so many people fear? Maybe it's just that Christians, like everyone else, are finding 21st century living harder and harder, so demand from their music and books these days less content and more feel-good?

Perhaps it's just the logical destination of a journey that started with my generation's post-modern suspicion of authority and 'facts'? What's more, our new breed of atheists have made such a song and dance about how rational they are, and how religion is 'The Enemy of Reason', that maybe some Christians have just given up fighting on intellectual grounds and accepted their opponent's description of themselves?

Maybe it's none or all of the above. Who knows?

What I do know is that as life goes on, I find that Christianity is robust both rationally and experientially. As my knowledge of God has grown, so has my very direct experience of Him - I could tell you some stories. Atheism may have explanations as to how the world began and why we behave the way we do, but it cannot explain my life.

Having a rational, coherent and consistent faith is not an optional extra. We can't give up on it just because it's 'too hard'. We've probably all met Christians who check their brain in on a Sunday and pick it up again in time for work on Monday morning.

But equally, we've probably all met Christians who live in their heads, for whom their faith is primarily an intellectual exercise and makes little, if any, difference in day-to-day life. Remember – It's not like modernity was so great in the first place, with it's intellectual snobbery and belittling of experience.

God makes sense, and without Him, my experiences don't.

Perhaps if we valued the rational foundations of our faith more, we might be more interested in books and songs that stimulate our intellect. But equally, perhaps if we expected more of God, and hungered to genuinely experience Him, we might have more than songs and colouring-in books to help us cope with stress and fear.

2017 is coming. Ask yourself which aspect of your relationship with God is lacking – reason or experience – and think about what steps you can actually take, what prayer you can actually persistently pray, to strengthen that part of your faith.

Natural Words and Spiritual Words

05 January 2017

Sometimes I'll talk to someone about how things are going, and they'll say something like:

"When she was out walking the dog, Sheila noticed that the family a couple of doors down was selling their car. So, we bought it for a good price. It turned out to be really convenient."

So far, so good. Two normal human beings having a normal human conversation. However, what perplexes me is that in certain company the above phrase becomes the following:

"Thankfully, the Lord provided a replacement at an almost miraculous price. It was a real answer to prayer!"

It's not the language that I have a problem with, it's the inconsistency. There are people who rarely talk about 'answers to prayer' or use phrases like 'The Lord provided…' except when they're writing a prayer letter. It's like there's an unspoken rule that when you're reporting to a group of Christians, you need to run everything through an English to

Christianese translator first. Notice how in the second, the poor dog isn't holy enough to get a mention.

There shouldn't be a dichotomy between our day-to-day persona and who we are when we're being a 'Christian'. We were not made to be two different people. It's not healthy for us, and it's not particularly honouring to God. It's not right that we spend most of our lives communicating like reasonable human beings, and then in certain circumstances become scary religious androids.

Cornerstone had a saying – "Let your natural life be spiritual and your spiritual life natural." Like most organisations, Cornerstone was not immune to using buzzwords, but I found that many members of Cornerstone did have a very natural way of talking about their faith, without needing to resort to Christian keywords or jargon. There was something concrete about the way they talked. Something down-to-earth. Something fair dinkum.

Some people are normal most of the time, but whey they talk about their faith they make such an effort to sound 'spiritual' that they become insubstantial, like a phantom that you could just push your hand through, if you know what I mean. Faith is not supposed to be that kind of 'spiritual'. It's supposed to be mundane, in the original sense of the word, so routine, so solid that when the world runs face-first into it it's left with a headache.

The Rich Man and the Farmer

12 January 2017

There was once a rich man who owned many wonderful and precious things, and he loved those things greatly. There was, however, one thing that he loved more than all of his possessions, all of his wealth, and that was himself.

One day, the rich man sent word throughout the kingdom.

"I own treasures that any man would desire, but surely the most amazing and precious thing is myself, the man who owns all of these treasures. If anyone can bring me a great and beautiful prize that I will love more than I love myself, then I will give this person everything that I own, and pass my great wealth on to them."

People came from far and wide to bring something that the rich man would love more than himself. Merchants brought rare and exotic items from the far corners of the world, noblemen brought their beautiful daughters, musicians brought angelic songs, but the rich man loved none of these things more than he loved himself.

One day, a farmer visited his court.

"Have you brought me something that I will love more than myself?" the rich man said.

"I have, my lord," said the farmer.

"What is it?" said the rich man.

The farmer opened his hand, and in the middle was a small seed.

"What is that? A seed?" The rich man laughed. "I have seen fantastic seeds, brought from the far corners of the world, and you think that one small, plain seed will impress me?"

"It is not the seed, my lord," said the farmer, "but rather it is what the seed becomes."

"And what is that?"

"I will show you, my lord."

The farmer planted the seed in the corner of one of the rich man's gardens and left. The rich man thought nothing more of it.

Many years passed, and still the rich man loved himself more than anything else. One day, the farmer returned.

"Who are you?" the rich man said.

"I am the farmer who brought you a seed many years ago, my lord."

"Oh yes, I remember. Well, the years have not been kind to you. Farming must be a tiresome work."

The farmer just smiled.

"Would you like to see what has become of the seed, my lord?"

"Very well," said the rich man.

The farmer took the rich man to the corner of the garden where he had planted the seed, and there stood a beautiful apple tree. But the rich man wasn't impressed.

"What is that? An apple tree? I have orchards full of the things, as well as amazing and exotic plants from the far corners of the word, and you think an apple tree will impress me?"

"It is not the tree, my lord," said the farmer, "but rather it is what the tree gives us."

"And what is that?"

"I will show you, my lord."

The farmer reached up and plucked a plump, ripe apple from one the branches.

"An apple? I told you that I have orchards and groves! I have succulent fruits and choice vegetables from the far corners of the world, and you think a mere apple will impress me?"

"It is not the apple, my lord," said the farmer, "but rather it is what is inside the apple."

"And what is that?"

The farmer took a bite from the apple, and then plucked a small seed from its middle, a seed that looked identical to the one that he had bought the rich man all those years ago.

"A seed? What is so…" began the rich man, but then he stopped, and he understood.

He loved himself more than anything, but he too was only as temporary as his possessions. If there was anything that he should love more, it was God, who was eternal like the apple seed, and the source of all good things.

The rich man was ashamed.

"You have shown me the folly of my pride. Everything I have is yours."

"No, my lord," said the farmer. "Nothing that any of us have is really ours."

The rich man understood this too, and he decreed that all of his possessions should be sold and the proceeds divided among the poor.

The rich man was no longer a rich man, but he considered himself a wiser man, and a better man, and nothing brought him greater pleasure.

Writer's Block, Inspiration and Stuff Like That

19 January 2017

I'm a lazy writer. Like many, I suppose, I depend on that mythical beast Inspiration to get me started, but when that endangered species is absent, then my passion and the words dry up. A huge part of writing is really just about discipline, and that's my least favourite part. When the dreams are flowing, it's all fine, but when I can't squeeze a single word that I'm happy with onto paper then it's not fine. I've been lacking inspiration for months now. You might call it Writer's Block. Every now and then I'll vomit out something passable, usually for the blog, but as for long-term projects? That well is currently dry.

The blog is good in that regard, because there's some weekly discipline right there. I hate it sometimes, but then that's how I feel about a good many things that are of benefit to my health.

So what's the point of me, then? Surely a writer who isn't writing is about as much use as a surgeon who's had his head cut off. Gosh, that was a clumsy comparison, wasn't it? This is what I mean, about the lack of inspiration.

I've been wondering recently what's next for the writing. Maybe the shortage of fruit over the past few months means it's time to call it a day. From a financial perspective, I can tell you that not writing pays even less than writing. So what happens when you're a writer who isn't writing? What does that mean?

Not much, to be honest. Because I know a secret. I'm not really a writer. I never was. I'm a son of God. That's who I am. So, whether I'm a son of God who writes, or a son of God who doesn't write, it doesn't really matter. The truly important thing remains the same in both those states, and that's not going to change.

Of course I'm not going to hang up my quill. Not yet. Writing is a spiritual discipline, and spiritual disciplines involve deserts as well as rivers. I just know that it's important for me to not forget that my identity is never, *never*, really about what I do. A curse of manhood is how we are conditioned to tie our identity to our job. It's one of the first questions that men ask each other when we meet: "And what do *you* do?" It establishes the pecking order. Lets you know whether or not you're talking to a *proper* man. We are what we do. That's what we think. But that's just another lie. We are who God says we are. Full stop.

Those desert periods are fruitful too. Those are the times when we learn some beautiful truths. We didn't realise they were beautiful before, but in the desert they're no longer forced to compete for our attention.

People say that you should follow your dreams. I say that you should follow God's dreams. They're bigger and better than yours, and wilder than you can imagine.

No. I think I'll keep writing, thank you very much.

Handling the Psalms with Care

26 January 2017

It's been said that the Bible is a record of God speaking to Man, but the Psalms are a record of Man speaking to God. This, I think, is one of the reasons why they have a universal appeal. Psalm 23 is the *Amazing Grace* of the Bible; it's the one that everyone knows. The power of the Psalms is that they put into words the inner music of the human soul. Whatever is going on in you, there's a Psalm that you can read and say, "Me too!"

For this reason, I'm always wary when people build theological castles on Psalmic foundations. The usual rules of hermeneutics apply, of course. The Psalms are poetry, therefore they are full of vibrant metaphors and hyperbole. They weren't written to justify doctrine, and therefore we need to be careful if we rely on the Psalms to proof-text our theology. But that's not the only reason to handle them with care.

The Psalms are the overflow of the heart. Anguish, joy, love, fear, depression – it's all there. We miss the point if we think that the Psalms are just sitting there waiting to be dissected with surgical

41

precision by our literary tools. If I write a love letter to my wife I don't expect her to respond by finding fault with my grammar and punctuation. In the same way, if we approach the Psalms with logic as our guide, we do them violence. Raw cries of the heart will always unsettle those who prefer a rigid blueprint to genuine trust.

In *Sermons in Solitary Confinement*, Richard Wurmbrand writes about a conversation that he had with the Russian pastor of an underground church. The pastor was uneducated, and had never even seen a complete New Testament. Wurmbrand took it upon himself to teach this man. He explained all that he could, talking about the Trinity, sin, the sacraments, the Church, and salvation. The Russian pastor listened intently, and when Wurmbrand had finished, he spoke.

"Have those," he said, "who thought out and wrote down these theological systems ever carried a cross?"

Wurmbrand was caught off guard by this question. The pastor went on.

"A man cannot think systematically even when he has something as mild as toothache. How can a man who is carrying a cross think systematically?"

When you read the Psalms, you are being invited into both the darkest and lightest places. Indeed, the Bible is full of such rich theological and systematic truths, but when you read the Psalms, God gives you a knowing wink and says, "This is my gift to you. Take off your shoes. You're on holy ground."

Nothing Good

02 February 2017

"Nothing good can come of this,"
said the man,
watching his neighbour leave his home
because he had heard a desert voice.

***

"Nothing good can come of this,"
said the woman,
as another desert stretched before her
and her children for another forty years.

***

"Nothing good can come of this,"
said the sailor,
as he watched the reluctant prophet
disappear beneath the waves.

***

"Nothing good can come of this,"
said yet another carpenter,
as he made yet another wooden cross
for yet another Roman crucifixion.

"Nothing good can come of this,"
said the scribe,
watching the loud-mouthed, uneducated fools
making wild claims in the temple courts.

***

"Nothing good can come of this,"
says the Voice of Common Sense.
Common Sense doesn't know
what it's talking about.

The Death of Character

09 February 2017

What do people want from their leaders? Reflecting on my own experiences in leadership and viewing the current political climate in the West makes me conclude that what we really want are leaders who think the same way as us. The personality and character of a leader is less important than whether or not he or she agrees with me on certain issues. We want leaders who are an extension of our opinions, a proxy who will do the things that we would do if we were in charge. "My will be done," we say.

Throughout the Bible it's the men and women who seek to please God that are regarded as ideal leaders – sometimes this meant that they actually stood against the crowd, who wanted nothing more than puppets. King David is held up as the rock that all great kings are hewn from, yet once that crown sat upon his head we hear a lot about his mistakes - adultery, murder, pride, not being a good father, and yet he is venerated because he was 'a man after God's own heart'. Despite the sorrow that he brought upon himself and others, the Kingdom of

Israel – the people under his care – are considered to have benefited from the reign of a man who tried, without always succeeding, to be a particular type of man rather than to achieve certain things.

I've read a lot of books, seen a few good leaders in action and made some first-rate mistakes of my own as a leader, and I can tell you that what you really need is someone with character. You want someone with integrity, who will do what is right rather than what you want; someone who is the same behind closed doors as they are in front of the cameras. That's a good leader. Where are all the good leaders these days? Instead we have pale imitations, ratings chasers, chameleons who change their message as often as they change their underpants. We have criminals and snake oil salesmen, name callers and blame throwers, self-seekers and egotists. What's bizarre is that these are the leaders we have chosen. In the City and in the Church, we get the leaders that we deserve.

There's no point asking God for good leaders if we're going to continue to choose to follow the ones that don't have noble character.

Experiences of Leadership

16 February 2017

My post last week got me thinking about some of my own experiences in leadership. Sometimes a leader needs to be a good negotiator, a good speaker, a good manager, or a good accountant. Sometimes there are things that can only be done by a good person.

We'd been at Canowindra for three years when the Cornerstone leadership asked the Dean of the campus to lead a new team in Orange. They asked me to become the new Dean. I said yes. I would be leading some of the best men and women I had ever met, but it had been hard work and we were already fragile. I really believed that we could get better and succeed, and that I could be a part of that. It turned out that the damage that had been done was worse than I'd thought, and it ran deeper than I think any of us had known. I don't remember when I first realised that the staff at Canowindra were carrying a mortal wound – possibly early on in my second year as Dean – but we struggled on, because we were doing good things and we were good people and we had hope.

One day I was at the poplars (my Australian Thin Place) and was interrogating God as to what was going on, and why he'd put me in this situation. I felt like God said to me, "Who else could do it? Who else could survive?" It made me laugh, the thought that God had put me at the helm not because of my ability and leadership skills, but because my faith was robust enough to survive the inevitable crash. It was like He was saying, "You can't fix this, James. You haven't got the skills or experience to save this, but you have one redeeming feature. When it all goes belly-up, I at least know that you're not going to throw your toys out of the pram and walk away from your faith."

So, after three years of struggling along, we – as a team – reached a point where we couldn't go on. They replaced us with younger and more enthusiastic people. My original team, We Happy Few, limped away to the four corners of the globe, battered and bruised. For all of us it seemed like a good point at which to re-evaluate our relationship with Cornerstone. Ruth and I seriously considered staying on as part of a different community, but eventually concluded that it was time to come home.

And God was right. I was broken, but not destroyed. I still walk with a limp, but at least I'm still walking. I gladly forgave, my relationship with God was strengthened, and I have nothing but love and gratitude for Cornerstone and the men and women I served with and under. I don't think that I did a particularly good job, but I did the job, and that was all that was asked of me I think. I'm sure that my "Well done, good and faithful servant" is in the pipeline.

The other day I watched a Kevin Costner film about coastguard rescue swimmers, *The Guardian*. A recurring question in that film was, "What do you do when you can't save them all?" It's like being a leader. You can't solve all the problems. There will be situations that you just can't fix or turn around. Some of them might even be fatal. At that point, you'd better hope that you're being led by a good person, because it takes a strong character to fail well.

The Road to Hell...

23 February 2017

I saw a man throwing a child at the sun.

"Why are you doing that?" I said.

"I'm helping him. He told me that he was cold," the man said.

I looked at the bruised child on the floor.

"I think he needs to go to the hospital," I said.

"Sure," said the man, lifting the child above his head once more. "Which direction is the hospital?"

Getting their Attention

02 March 2017

*A*n actor and a preacher were discussing their work. "What I don't understand," said the preacher, "is why my congregation will come to one of your performances and sit for hours, engaged and alert the whole time, while I can hardly get them to stay awake during one of my twenty minute sermons."

"Maybe," said the actor, "it's because I present fiction as though it were the truth, and you present the truth as though it were fiction."

When I first started my preaching journey, the received wisdom was that you needed to get the congregation's attention immediately. It makes sense. You don't have long before people switch off – some research suggests that you have under ten seconds to get them engaged. Back then the tool you used was to start your sermon with something interesting or humourous; you use something that people will actually want to listen to, like a story or a joke. As far as I can tell, this is still common practice. I sometimes start a sermon this way – but not all the time. It's right to make an effort to be engaging, but there's a difference between being intriguing and merely being entertaining.

There's nothing wrong with starting your sermon with a story, but if you do it every week then it can become a problem. When a humourous anecdote is your *modus operandi* then people expect it: "Good old Reverend so and so. Always starts with a funny story." People listen, but you're just delaying the inevitable. They'll still switch off, but they'll just wait until after the punchline. Then you're not a preacher – your words have no power. You're just an entertainer.

We are preaching the words of eternal life, using a text that has caused revolutions, shaken souls and brought hope and encouragement to millions over the millennia, and we think that we need to use anecdotes to get people's attention? People don't come to church to be amused (from the Greek *'a muse'*, literally *'without thought'*). They come to meet God and to be equipped to live their lives well, and if that's not why they come, I still act as though it is. The sermon should be one of the places where this can happen. If people quickly get the impression that what you are going to say to them this morning will actually have *meaning*, that it will make a difference to their lives, then you'll have their attention – and you'll keep it.

I'm definitely not saying there's no place for humour, or stories, or observations in sermons. That would be ridiculous, especially coming from me. Those things are my bread and butter – but if that's all I bring to the table then I'm done with preaching. The best way to get a congregation's attention is to try to preach sermons that meet needs, answer the questions that people are actually asking, and (most importantly) create space for the Holy Spirit to do His thing. If we can do that, we'll have no problems getting their attention.

Eight Seductive Narratives

9 March 2017

One: Christians should never ever cause trouble.

Two: The harder you work, the more God owes you.

Three: Spiritual warfare is no concern of mine.

Four: Jesus' job is to understand me, not to make demands on me.

Five: Because God is sovereign, it's OK for me to be spiritually lazy.

Six: The purpose of Christian youth work is to keep my children away from drink and drugs, not to put dangerous and radical ideas into their heads.

Seven: First, I sort out my security, then I see what God wants.

Eight: What I choose to watch and listen to has no affect on my thinking.

What's Important to God?

16 March 2017

There was this one time when I was asked to visit a friend of mine who was in hospital. Let me clarify what I mean by 'in hospital'. He was actually in the hospital's locked ward. He'd had a psychotic episode and been sectioned. So I went to visit him, and I sat with him in the secure unit. I was out of my depth, which is where I spend a lot of my time. He asked me to read to him, from the Psalms, so that's what I did. That's all I did. For half an hour I just sat and read from the Psalms while he wept beside me. Then I went home to my family.

I know that I have public gifts, the sort of gifts that draw attention. I have been told that I preach eloquently and, sometimes, powerfully. I know that there are those who have been influenced by my teaching. It's been said that I write well, and that I am a gifted communicator. But I think about that time in the locked ward, and I have a sneaking suspicion that, even if I were to live to be one hundred years old, I will never do anything as important as that ever again.

A Psalm of the Storm

23 March 2017

Crunching along the path,
the black skies reflect
on how easily I mislay my peace:
Like a five pence coin, a TV remote
or a needle in a haystack.

They used to call it the Pax Deus.
Better it is,
than the Pax so-called
of Romana, Britannica, or the
Americana we have these days.

Passing all understanding makes it fragile.
Inevitably broken,
like a light bulb in your pocket.
Funny how it still seems to work
when the room goes dark.

The river at my side grumbles,
as does my heart.
And my mind?
It just comes along for the ride
as the clouds form an angry congregation.

And on days like these,
when I can't decide
if my soul is cold or warm,
I hurl my praise in Your direction,
the God of the sun and the storm.

The World Waits with Baited Breath

30 March 2017

I't's easy to hold the Church up as a good argument for atheism. Our shame is not that we have been exceptionally bad, but rather that we haven't been exceptionally good. But you can't shake off the Holy Spirit that easily. Even after two thousand years, the World still expects us to keep Jesus' promises. After all, you can't be disappointed with something unless you'd hoped that it would be better, right? The problem is not that Christianity is bad, but rather that we have made a bad job of Christianity. I believe that even the most die-hard atheist still expects the followers of Jesus to be different to the rest of society - to be good where others are not.

Dennis Prager, a Jewish-American conservative commentator, believes that, regardless of what people think of religion, there remains in Western culture an expectation that faith should make a difference to behaviour. He tries to prove this by asking people to picture something particular.

Imagine that late one night you are walking down an alley in a major city. The dim street lights illuminate your car at the other end of the alleyway. Suddenly, a group of boisterous young men turn the corner and start walking down the alley towards you.

Once the listener has this scene in his mind, Prager asks this question: Would you feel safer if you knew that those young men had just come from a Bible study?

Prager says that he has never had anyone answer "No."

So, that's the good news. People are just waiting for you to prove them right. Even now they still assume that you will be different. The best thing to do is to live in such a way that our children, our children's children and our children's children's children will benefit from the same expectation.

Creed

06 April 2017

I believe in God the Father, the creator of the world and everything in it.

I believe that He has guided His people over the years, with many miraculous signs.

I believe that He parted the Red Sea, provided manna from heaven and led Israel as pillars of smoke and fire.

I believe in Jesus Christ, the God with us.

I believe that through His life and death, God has worked salvation for all humanity.

I believe that Jesus rose from the dead, and so delivered the ultimate "Take that!" to the forces of evil.

I believe that death is defeated, and life is eternal.

I believe in the Holy Spirit, the God in us.

I believe these things, because they are easy to believe from a distance.

But I don't believe that He is that committed to using me to bring His kingdom on earth.

I don't believe that He has much interest in my day-to-day life,
or that He even has much to say,

and if He did, He certainly wouldn't do it through that person.

I don't believe that God will part my Red Sea, nor do I expect
Him to provide manna, or to lead me.

I don't believe, in the grand scheme of things, that it matters
much what I do.

And I don't believe that He really means what He says.

Amen.

What if it's Already Happened?

13 April 2017

Easter is a topsy-turvey time. Everything is back-to-front. Suffering brings salvation, death brings life; the established order of things is turned on its head. Yet we spend so much of our time and energy trying to make things work in a world where we believe that death is stronger than life and that despair is greater than hope.

How much of our well-being do we invest in worry? How often does the thing that we fear never actually happen? What about the times when we worry about something we *think* has happened, only to find out that it didn't happen after all? How tiring it is to live in a world where God is a footnote rather than the title.

In the last chapter of Luke we read about two of Jesus' followers. They're taking a long stroll, discussing the events of the past few days and the rumours of resurrection. Suddenly, they're joined by a stranger. He's not really a stranger, but they don't recognise him because they hadn't quite joined the topsy-turvey revolution yet. They tell this stranger their story of disappointment. "Jesus has been crucified," they say, "but we had hoped that he would be the one to redeem Israel."

The two travellers were living under the burden of false disappointment. They thought that their hope was an illusion, when it turned out that it was reality – a reality that was standing right in front of them.

This is the way to live back-to-front in our world, the way to get some of the Easter thinking into our heads. Instead of worrying about things that might never happen, start thinking about all the things that you hope for, and ask yourself if maybe some of them *have already happened.*

Writers Wot Have Influenced Me – Part 5 of 4 Flannery O'Connor

20 April 2017

"She had never given much thought to the devil for she felt that religion was essentially for those people who didn't have the brains to avoid evil without it. For people like herself, for people of gumption, it was a social occasion providing the opportunity to sing; but if she had ever given it much thought, she would have considered the devil the head of it and God the hanger-on. With the coming of these displaced people, she was obliged to give new thought to a good many things."

The Displaced Person, Flannery O'Connor

I won't be surprised if many of you are asking, "Who is Flannery O'Connor, and is that his real name?" Well, *she* was an American author. She died of Lupus in 1964, aged a mere 39, yet is regarded as one of the most influential writers to ever come out of the American South.

Her stories are invariably set in that particular region of the United States, and she was quite willing to tackle sensitive themes in an insensitive time - notably racism. However, what was quite noticeable to me about her writing was that she clearly had a deep understanding of human nature. As grotesque as some of her characters are, they are not only believable, but also relatable. That's some achievement.

The thing about her that I've found particularly inspiring is this: Many of her stories contain explicit Christian themes, written about subtly but powerfully. She wrote about a world that, as Gerard Manley Hopkins put it, is 'charged with the grandeur of God'. She writes about grace and redemption and the fact that, in her own words, "grace changes us and the change is painful."

I think it's clear from her writing that she was dissatisfied with the particular brand of fundamentalist Protestantism she encountered in the Deep South, obviously seeing too little of the grace of Christ and too much godless moralism, perhaps epitomised in stories like *The River* and *The Displaced Person* (which, whether she meant it or not, is almost a parable of the gospel itself). That is to be expected, as she was a devout Roman Catholic, which no doubt put her in a minority amongst the people she grew up with.

I've been making my way through her *Complete Stories*, and although the first few are a bit of a slog, everything from *Enoch and the Gorilla* onwards has been, so far, fantastic.

I suppose that I admire her refusal to be bullied, neither by her heritage nor by that culture of Western fiction which is much happier when God is either non-existent or the villain of the piece. She is, I think, more proof that the world actually finds something irresistible about the gospel, and will happily sit and listen to someone who communicates it with skill. She is one of those writers whose work both inspires me and makes me feel inadequate. She was dead by my age, so I've got a lot of catching up to do.

Two Types of Fire

27 April 2017

God has given me two types of inner fire.

A few months after I became a Christian I was attending a men's prayer breakfast at my church. During prayer, I experienced what I can only describe as a warm, tingling sensation in my chest. The best effort to put it into words can be found in the Bible, on the lips of one of my older brothers as he and a friend talked about their encounter with the risen Jesus: "Were not our hearts burning within us while he explained the Scriptures to us?" It's happened to me frequently over the years, mostly during prayer. It's comforting rather than anything else, and I've come to associate it with an awareness of the Holy Spirit. It's just one of those practical, concrete hooks on which I can hang my faith.

The other fire, however, is different. It's what I might call 'the squirming inferno'. Again, the best way to describe it can be found in the Bible, this time as the prophet Jeremiah complains. Frustrated by how much trouble God had caused him, he handed in his notice. "Find yourself another prophet," he says to the divine. But it's not that simple, and Jeremiah discovers that the message of God will not be smothered. It was, he said, like a fire in his bones. Sometimes (more often than I would like) I find myself restless, and tortured by the feeling that there is some important truth I should be getting out there. The problem is that it's a time-consuming, difficult and painful process to set it free. Often it's like realising that its your job to slay a giant dragon, and not even knowing how to begin. Those are the worst times. The only way to keep it quiet is to actually try and do something with it, however feeble my efforts, but it's never satisfied. I don't think I'll ever be able to completely pay off its debt – the squirming inferno is probably here to stay.

They're both from God. One is His way of saying, "I love you, and I am always with you"; the other is His way of saying, "But I'm not going to let you get away with being lazy." I am loved, but I *am* lazy. I am genuinely thankful for both of these flames, because I need the warmth *and* the refining.

Eight Things that Made me Laugh Out Loud

04 May 2017

I've spent a long time this week working on a blog post about popularity, but I've decided that I don't want to post it. It might have been profound, but it was also quite negative. Being the melancholy sort that I am, I have a tendency to go full Old Testament Prophet sometimes, and it's not good for me, you or the Kingdom of God if all I do is complain. After all, there's a reason why we commemorate architects and not demolitions experts. What's the point of being a follower of Jesus if you can't lose yourself in laughter every now and then?

So, instead, here is a list of eight things that have made me laugh out loud:

1. The time I was with my children at a playground and I went down the slide, but my t-shirt got caught at the top of the slide, leaving me dangling halfway down the slide with a ripped t-shirt around my upper chest and neck.

2. *Phil's Tribute* – a dance video that Sam and Ethan prepared for our 2011 end of year formal at Cornerstone Canowindra.

3. Walking past Reid and Calvin's bedroom, and overhearing Reid telling Calvin about a chimpanzee that was found guilty of a crime and sentenced to five years at Wingham Wildlife Park – complete with chimpanzee noises.

4. The time that my in-laws (Max & Sue) sent some flowers to my parents, and they arrived with a card that read 'From Mac and Sue'.

5. That bit in *Adventure Time* where Ice King says, "Without Gunter, I'll be all alone. You see, I'm a widower." and Doctor Princess says, "Oh, I'm sorry. How did your wife die?" and Ice King says, "Ohh…Is that what that means?"

6. My friend Terry's story about the time he was using a cubicle in a public toilet, and he heard someone else coming in, and he assumed it was one of his friends who had been waiting outside and he yelled out in a weird squeaky

voice, "No, no, go away!" then he heard a voice he didn't recognise say, "Uhh...sorry mate." and Terry had to reply "That's alright." in the same weird squeaky voice that he'd just used.

7. Sam, Mark and Darren on the hamster wheel at the playground in Blayney.

8. The video footage of me on a motorbike, pootling along, suddenly accelerating out of control and crashing into a fence while my wife, who was on the video camera, cackles like a witch in the background.

"Should we not see that the lines of laughter about the eyes
are just as much marks of faith
as are the lines of seriousness and care?"

Helmut Thielicke

In Gratitude for Dianne Tyson

11 May 2017

I didn't ever meet Dianne, but that didn't matter. She didn't even reach sixty, but that didn't matter either. A lot of things about Dianne didn't seem to matter. The fact that she was plagued with crippling health problems and constant pain - that didn't matter either. She had a lot to bitter about, but she didn't let those things matter.

She spoke openly about her suffering, but she was a fine example of someone who didn't let herself be defined by the things that had happened to her, but instead *redefined* those things in the light of who God had made her to be. She was physically inactive, but spiritually active. Not just spiritually active, I suppose, but spiritually vibrant; spiritually contagious even. For those of you who don't know, she prayed faithfully for me and many others on a regular basis, and those prayers *did* matter. When Dianne phoned you and said, "I was praying for you yesterday and I felt like God was saying…", well, you'd better have listened. She was the sort of person that caused Satan to break out into a cold sweat. That may sound a touch melodramatic, but I have experienced first hand how God used her to thwart the enemy's little schemes, and I know I'm not the only one.

Of course, like all men and women cut from that beautiful cloth, she would be nonplussed and embarrassed to read such things written about herself, but that's all part of the deal, isn't it? Brokenness and humility are both the things that God uses, and the things that prevent us from getting carried away by our usefulness.

I didn't ever meet Dianne, but I will miss her and part of me wishes she was still here. We are poorer without her and there's a lot of work still to be done, but she's earned her rest.

One day I'll thank her face to face, because – one day – we'll have that first meeting.

The Cost of Discipleship

18 May 2017

"*Go away!*" *squealed the Ghost.* "*Go away! Can't you see I want to be left alone?*"

"*But you need help,*" *said the Solid One.*

"*If you have the least trace of decent feeling left,*" *said the Ghost,* "*you'll keep away. I don't want help. I want to be left alone…*"

The Great Divorce, C.S. Lewis

'Insufficient' is not a word that good Evangelicals would typically apply to Jesus' death, but Paul wasn't so squeamish. Notice what he tells the Colossians: 'Now I rejoice in what was suffered for you, and I fill up in my flesh what is lacking in regard to Christ's afflictions, for the sake of his body, which is the Church.'

Paul is not, of course, suggesting that we need more than Jesus to restore our relationship with the Father, rather he is saying, "Jesus' suffering may bring salvation, but it does not necessarily bring maturity. Spiritual growth doesn't just happen. You need someone to get alongside you and teach you, feed you and change your dirty nappies. That's the job that I've taken on for the Church, and let me tell you this: *It's a costly business."*

That's the hidden cost of discipleship. In our immaturity we don't realise that the men and women who invest in us, and help us get to know God better, can only do so by giving up something of themselves. I think about the time people spent with me rather than doing something infinitely preferable; I think about the suffering that others went through so that I could be spared some of the same pain; I think about those who spend an hour on Sunday mornings helping my children get to know God.

But this reliance on one another, rather than just God, isn't some oversight on His part; some side effect of sin. It's the divine core of discipleship. God wouldn't have it any other way. He's terribly keen on interdependence, you know. It's what He wants, for us to need others; it's the inbuilt 'flaw' that forces us into relationships – forces us to emulate the Trinity. If Jesus' life, death and resurrection were sufficient not just for salvation, but made our spiritual growth inevitable, then we wouldn't need community. We could retreat to our monastic cells and just sit around, waiting for sanctification to kick in. God's not going to give us that excuse. So He made it that for me to grow, I need people, and those people have to pay a debt of love. And then He made it so that I have to do the same for others. Clever. That's probably why Paul felt able to rejoice in this particular cost of discipleship.

Creating Life

25 May 2017

I really needed my character to make that phone call, but it just wasn't working. The story demanded that he pick up the phone and dial those numbers, but it didn't feel right. So what do I do now, when I have a story, but a character who doesn't want to play ball? "All right," I said to my character, "what do you want to do then?" You can imagine my shock and disappointment when he took that scrap of paper with the phone number on it, scrunched it up and threw it in the bin. "What are you doing?" I said, "I need you to phone that number!" But it was no good. He wasn't going to make the call.

Once I'd recovered, I realised that it made sense. This character, the person that he was, wouldn't make the call. Not yet. So he didn't, and I was left at a loose end. Instead of following the plot, we went on a detour and did something else for a while. Then several pages later, he was pulling that piece of paper out of the bin so that he could make the call, all of his own accord. The story was back on track. We got there eventually, but he had to be ready.

A lot of writers advocate this – you don't write the story, you write the characters and then let them decide on the story. When it works you have a tale that is internally consistent and compelling, but you have to know your characters. They have to be real people who can tell you what they would say and do and feel. You just listen, and put it on paper.

I know there are some writers who don't even have a story when they start. They just have a bunch of fleshed-out characters and a starting situation (what Robert McKee would call an 'Inciting Incident'), and see where it all goes. I'm not quite like that. I like to have an end goal in mind, but it definitely works better when I let the characters get me there, rather than railroad them towards their destiny. Of course, that means surrendering some control.

Letting the life that you have created exercise free will is hard work, and riskier than the alternative, but it creates a richer story and leads to a greater reward.

Memento – Part One

01 June 2017

*M*emento is a film about Leonard's search for the enigmatic 'John G' – the man who killed his wife. The challenge for Leonard (played by Mike from *Neighbours*) is that he suffers from short-term memory loss. This throws a spanner in the works of his detectoring. He gets around this inconvenience with a collection of Polaroid photographs and a mass of tattoos that remind him of important snippets of information he has gleaned over the years. Of course, him constantly having to make sense of all this information anew is part of where the film's twists and turns come from.

I have to say that I am quite taken with the idea of having really important things that I need to remember tattooed on myself. I'm aware of my own short-term memory loss that sees me forgetting who I really am, and playing the wrong game. If it was up to me, I'd go full-*Memento* and cover myself with black ink – **FACT 1: You are a Son of God FACT 2: Remember that God thinks everyone you meet was worth the life of Jesus** and so on. Ruth won't let me do this, and that's fair enough. It's one of many reasons why she's good to have around. It's a shame though, as my middle-aged weight gain is beginning to show, so I've got plenty of room on my slowly-expanding canvas for some really important truths. So, I have to think of other less drastic ways to remember important things, because I really don't want to forget.

Interestingly though, I think that there are such things as hidden tattoos, but more on that next week...

Memento – Part Two

08 June 2017

Most of us get bruised as we make our way through this world. Sometimes those bruises take a long time to heal, and might leave us tender and scarred beneath the surface. In *Memento*, Leonard lets his tattoos and notes guide him. He trusts them completely, and they become his truth. In the same way, we sometimes let our wounds control our actions and outlook on life. The world is full of people who let their scars do the talking.

I find it interesting that the risen Jesus still had the wounds from his crucifixion. It makes me speculate: perhaps those wounds that we have suffered in service to God will be a part of our perfect resurrection body. Our images of heaven might feature beautiful men and women with perfect teeth and unblemished skin, but I wonder if the truth might be different. Perhaps Paul, and all those who can say with him that they "…bear on my body the marks of Jesus…" might still have those wounds in heaven and – far from being a sign of imperfection and suffering – they might be a badge of honour.

But, as I was saying, sometimes those wounds are hidden; there are unseen scars. They count too. As I hinted at above, it's the unseen tattoos that tend to have the most control over us. I've acquired a few cuts and grazes on my soul in my attempts to follow Jesus, but I don't want them to shape me negatively. Instead I try to think of them a bit like *Memento* tattoos. They spell out words too – words like *obedient* and *owned by God* and *faithful*. After all, I wouldn't have got them if it wasn't for the risks I've taken in trying to serve Him. I don't want to ignore them, or try to pretend that they're not there, but neither do I want to relate to the world out of hurts and disappointments. Paul, the master of being wounded both by and for God, understood, I think, that these internal tattoos were sacraments – reminders of the divine – when he said, "...I delight in weaknesses, insults, hardships, in persecutions, in difficulties, for when I am weak, then I am strong."

Silence in Heaven

15 June 2017

Sometimes I don't have any words, which can be a bit awkward because words are supposed to be *my thing*. But sometimes, after the past couple of weeks, with politics and faith, terrorism and flames, there are no words. All I have is silence.

It makes me think of the beginning of Revelation chapter 8, when the seventh seal is opened and there is silence in heaven for half an hour. Did you know that sometimes heaven is silent too? If you're one of those people who can't bear silence, who has to fill a void with words, no matter how banal or ill chosen, then you might want to get some practice in being silent – there will come a time when words aren't welcome.

Even in God's presence, there are times when no words will do. I like that. When I have nothing to say, I don't need to say anything, because the citizens of heaven know what it is like to have no words.

My Philosophy of Communication

22 June 2017

I sn't it nice when you discover that someone has put into words something that you already knew to be true on an instinctual level? A few years ago I stumbled upon a quote that resonated with my soul. As a preacher/teacher, I sort of knew what I was trying to do – I wasn't really so interested in 'educating' as I was in 'inspiring'. However, 'Inspiring' is not usually listed as a Learning Outcome on many course outlines, much to my disappointment.

What I had realised from my own life is that inspiring someone is often better than just educating, simply because inspiration is its own motivation. Teaching someone how to read the Bible is good, but it won't necessarily lead to more Bibles being read. *Inspiring* someone to read the Bible? Well, that's a different matter. People who are motivated to do something will find ways of doing it, even if they haven't been taught how to. Of course, the best preaching/teaching does both – teaches you how to do something *and* motivates you to do it. I might be in a minority here, but if I can only do one of those things I'll plump for inspiration every time. When I look back on my life, it's been my desire to follow Christ that has carried me through the dry, hard, lonely times. God can make up for the shortfall of ignorance, but He can't do anything with a cold heart.

Anyway, the quote. It's from a French writer and pilot called Antoine de Saint-Expury:

"If you want to build a ship, don't drum up the men to gather wood, divide the work, and give orders. Instead teach them to yearn for the vast and endless sea."

How much better would the quality of our faith be if we had not taught people 'The Christian Way to Do Things', but instead had given them a hunger for God?

How Relationships Win Wars

29 June 2017

Speaking of boats (well, I was last week), I've been reading a book – Ben Wilson's *Empire of the Deep: The Rise and Fall of the British Navy*. It's a cracking read, for the three of us who are interested in British naval history. It's been interesting to read about Admiral Nelson, whose superlative performance in battle seemed to come down to the level of trust he'd built up with his officers, and that he'd earned the respect and love of his superbly disciplined sailors. In short, Nelson's success was down to how well he managed his relationships. That may be an oversimplification, but it's beyond dispute that he was loved by the men who served under him. Nelson understood, I think, that leadership has at least as much to do with relationships as it does to do with ability.

While reading this book, I was reminded of a story I'd once heard about Nelson's funeral. A quick internet search revealed that it was actually true.

Towards the end of the funeral service, sailors from *HMS Victory* were supposed to take the ship's colours and place them on a table. Instead, the sailors ripped a chunk from one of the flags and divided it between themselves to take away as a memento of the leader that they had loved.

I like this story. It's a simple act of love and memory, and it reminds me of something.

While they were eating, Jesus took bread; gave thanks and broke it, and gave it to his disciples, saying, "Take it; this is my body."

Mark 14:22

How to End the Gospel

06 July 2017

I admire Mark for the way that he ended his gospel: *"Trembling and bewildered, the women went out and fled from the tomb. They said nothing to anyone, because they were afraid."* Of course, most Bibles have another 11 verses stapled to the end which, as your footnotes will helpfully tell you, are not present in the earliest versions of Mark. Those verses were added over the years by scribes who couldn't bear the way that Mark had finished his book. "That's no way to end the story, Mark," they said. "Where's the good news? Where are the appearances of the risen Jesus, the promise of miracles and hope, the divine mission left to his disciples? You've got to have those in, Mark. It's called 'closure'. Don't you know anything about endings?"

On all these things, Mark is stubbornly silent. I admire his courage in letting the ending hang there, like a thread in the wind. I admire him, because he knew better than many of us how to end a story. I admire him because it's clear that he understood the gospel.

89

The resurrection was there. It didn't need to be explained. Instead Mark chose to end his story with something uncomfortable, dumped into your lap like an angry cat, unexpected, squirming and digging in its claws. "I'm not going to tell you what to think," he said. "I'm not going to fill in the gaps. I'm not going to answer your questions. I'm just going to tell you what happened, and leave it with you. You don't get to just listen with this one – it's too important for passivity. It's God's message, so what are you going to do with it?"

As much as I believe that the gospel makes sense of this Jekyll and Hyde world in which we live, I also know that if you go to God expecting answers you'll be disappointed. God doesn't usually answer questions – He asks them. When Mark tells the story of Jesus, he's not telling it to explain the world, he's telling it to make a demand on your life.

Mark understood that the message of Jesus was not just a fairy tale or a moralistic monologue. You have to do something with it, and that's why he leaves it unfinished. To force your hand. I admire him for that.

Naming & Shaming

13 July 2017

One of the many wise things that my counsellor, Derrick, said to me was, "You can humble yourself, or you can let God humble you. The first one is less painful."

How do you humble yourself? Well, that'll be between you and God, but it will require some decent soul-searching and some brutal honesty, I can tell you that.

Pride takes many forms, but one I know is the iron grip that says, "I will work my hardest at controlling how others, even God, see me. I will not admit anything that weakens my bargaining position. I will gladly speak generally about my failings and mistakes, but I will never be specific, not even to The One Who Already Knows."

If you know the name of your sin, but don't even have the humility to whisper it into God's ear then you're in a lot of trouble indeed. Not all pride is about drawing attention your way. There's a quiet pride that can't bring itself to confess, and it's a bigger killer than all those loud egotistical things that are so easy to identify and condemn.

In 1 Kings 21 we read about how Ahab, one of the worst kings in Israel's history, finds the threatened judgement postponed because he humbled himself. That's exactly what God noticed – that he *humbled himself*. He didn't wait for God to do it; he took responsibility for it himself. Never underestimate how willing God is to bless those who name their crimes, not just wanting to be forgiven, but wanting to be *better*.

Being humbled because of our sin is inevitable. It's better that we humble ourselves than wait for God to do it. A quick "Sorry, God!" may be enough to find forgiveness, but it may not be enough to find freedom.

No Rest for the Righteous

20 July 2017

If there's one thing I've learnt about spiritual warfare, it's that Satan is no gentleman. He isn't one to say, "Hey, James has had a really rough week. Let's go easy on him for the moment." Quite the opposite in fact. There may be times where the conflict is more overt, and I am more aware of it, but rarely do the guns actually stop.

As a preacher, I know that the build up to a sermon can be a time of conflict. The act of preparation, with the temptation to take shortcuts or play fast and loose with the truth, feels like a battle. When we're working towards something specific, we can be conscious of the spiritual struggle, wrestling with motives and prayer, but it's a mistake to think that *after* the event there's a ceasefire. As soon as the seed has landed on the path is the best time for the birds to swoop. The moment the preacher sits down is as good a time as any to push him into pride or drag him into despair.

However, as relentless as the Enemy is, God is even more so. The truth doesn't ever stop being true.

There is not a moment where resisting the devil doesn't cause him to flee from us. I don't stop being a child of God because I've had a bad week. We are always vulnerable to attack but, equally, the Enemy is always vulnerable to the truth.

...the More they Stay the Same

27 July 2017

Sometimes, I find it hard to remain totally committed to hope when a cursory look around provides plenty of reasons to despair. Thankfully, I *am* totally committed to hope. When I wrote *Look on the Bright Side* (which appears in *The Listening Book*) I was trying to nail my colours to the mast, the reasoning being that if I publicly put my beliefs on paper then I can't really give up without looking like a hypocrite. That's one way to make pride work *for* you.

It gets tricky when I'm going through the 'discouragement/despair' phase of my quarterly cycle (don't feel bad for me, I'm improving. It used to be a weekly cycle), but as G.K. Chesterton said, "Hope means hoping when things are hopeless, or it is no virtue at all... As long as matters are really hopeful, hope is mere flattery or platitude; it is only when everything is hopeless that hope begins to be a strength."

This morning I was reading Psalm 12. The first two verses resonated with me:

Help, Lord, for no one is faithful anymore;
  those who are loyal have vanished from the human race.
 Everyone lies to their neighbour;
  they flatter with their lips
  but harbour deception in their hearts.

There's a fellow pessimist at work right there. But, like me, the author was committed to hope precisely when things seemed hopeless. Having started with the bad news, he goes on to finish with the good news – a commitment to hope:

You, Lord, will keep the needy safe
  and will protect us forever from the wicked,
who freely strut about
  when what is vile is honoured by the human race.

It's the same in the following Psalm, which starts with the line "How long, O LORD? Will you forget me for ever?" and finishes a mere five verses later with "I will sing to the LORD, for he had been good to me."

In other words, all those hundreds of years ago, things were the same as they were today. There were plenty of things to get discouraged about, and plenty of opportunities to throw our hands up in the air and say "What are you doing, God?" but hope meant then – as it does now – ending your Psalm with a statement of trust and faith. And over all those hundreds of years, God has remained faithful and at work. Hope means being committed to this, even when the surrounding evidence contradicts it.

The Scraps from My Table

03 August 2017

I'm well aware that God doesn't always get the best of me. It's just that I'm busy, and I get tired, and – to be honest – there are plenty of things that I'd rather be spending my time and energy on than God. Of course, sometimes God does get my best, but not often. He gets what I feel like I can afford, which is much less than I can *actually* afford. I think that God is used to living on starvation rations.

I was thinking about this because I had been reminded about a story I was told once. It's about Jimmy Carter, who was the 39th President of the United States, and it's from his book *Why not the Best?*.

Apparently, Jimmy Carter was once asked to speak at a church in Preston, Georgia on the topic of 'Christian Witnessing'. Carter had been a member of Plains Baptist Church, which held an annual one-week outreach event where members of the church would visit people in their homes and share the gospel with them. He thought that, as part of his sermon, he would share from these experiences. He worked out that, in the fourteen years since leaving the Navy, he had visited 140 homes to tell people about Jesus. He felt quite proud of his efforts.

Then he started thinking about his 1966 campaign to be elected governor of Georgia. During the three month campaign he spent between sixteen and eighteen hours a day trying to reach as many people as possible. He calculated that he had met about 300,000 Georgians.

Carter was humbled by the comparison. In fourteen years he had reached 140 people for God, and in three months he had reached 300,000 people for himself.

God isn't the only one who has to make do with the scraps from my table — I also have a family that doesn't get the attention that they deserve. I don't think that there's any point feeling guilty about such things, but I do like to try and keep myself honest.

Soul Jar

10 August 2017

The soul is like a jar. It's probably made of clay. God seems to have a thing for clay.

Sometimes you go to someone's soul jar and it's empty. You look at the person, and you see the bitterness etched on his face and you roll your eyes. Words spring to mind: small-minded, tiny-hearted, empty soul. *No wonder*, you think, *that this soul jar is empty*. He is mean, wicked, horrible and anything poured into that jar would turn into vinegar the moment that it splashed against the sides.

But it doesn't work like that. The jar is not empty because of bitterness, but rather there is bitterness because the jar is empty.

Let me explain.

I watch a child dancing with breathless joy in the morning, while the world around me shouts "Fire and Fury!" and I think, *She doesn't understand and that's why she dances*. But then God taps me on the shoulder and says, "No, James, she *does* understand, and that's *why* she dances. You may have lost your way for a moment."

The jar starts full, but a swift kick here and a rough push there and a crack will show, and if we don't attend to it then the soul starts to leak out. If we don't watch those chips and fractures then we'll dry out. It might take years, but it'll happen.

"And it's not just your jar, James," says God. "You know what Fred Craddock says the rule for all big families is, don't you?"

"Yes, God," I reply. "The older ones help the younger ones."

"Good. Now fix your jar, and I can always top it up for you. And when you see someone else in danger of leaking out all over the place, you know what to do, don't you?"

"Yes, God," I say. "The older ones help the younger ones."

How's your jar?

How about the jars to your left and right?

Don't just watch the treasure leak out.

Who Knows What Failure Looks Like?

17 August 2017

One of the things about my life thus far is that it's so blatantly intertwined with God that it's impossible for me to answer a simple question like 'What do you do for a living?' without getting all spiritual if I so choose. However, when I try to explain the labyrinthian nonsense of the past twenty years I get a bit self-conscious. When I step outside myself and listen to what's coming out of my mouth, I worry that I just come across as an indecisive loser, saying "I did this for a while, but that didn't quite work out, so I went and did this..." *ad infinitum*. By now, it would have been nice to have found something that was a) sustainable and b) that I was actually *good* at.

The issue is that, precisely because it all involves God, I get a bit worried about how it reflects on Him. I'm not confident that I sound like a particularly good advert for a life committed to following Jesus. "Make God the centre of your life," I seem to be saying, "and you too can know the joy and freedom of repeated painful failure!" So, the temptation is to be not quite honest about the path I've walked, but only because I want to make God look good. Nothing wrong with that, right? Well, actually, it's all a bit ridiculous. It makes me think of a lyric from the Blindside song *Silver Speak* – "I'm an ant trying to protect my dinosaur friend."

There were once three men who were very concerned about making sure that God got a good rap. They had a friend who was going through a hard time, and was not shy about complaining. "Stop blaming God for *your* problems!" the three men said. "Who are you to drag His name down to your level. Pull yourself together!" They were angry with their friend, because he was making God look bad. In the end, God said to them, "You're angry on my behalf? Well, I'm angry with *you* because you have not spoken of me what is right, like my servant Job has."

I have to keep reminding myself, you see, that the journey I've been on has been *because* of God. I'm not someone who has tried a variety of career paths and not stuck at anything. I'm not even someone who "...just hasn't found his calling yet". I'm someone who has done what I believe God has asked me to do. The difficulty is that, in the Kingdom of

God, success looks a lot like failure, and failure looks a lot like success. A sick church is unable to distinguish between the two, and chases success, unaware that all the time it's just failure in a pretty wig. In the end, all God asks for is faithfulness. It's my job to live honestly, and not worry about how that makes God look.

The Sermon as Art

24 August 2017

Over the years, the line between writing a story and preparing a sermon has become blurred. These days, I tend to take the same approach with both, which means that I spend longer editing a sermon than writing it in the first place. I revisit it frequently, toying with the order of paragraphs, or searching for exactly the right image or turn of phrase.

It's not about 'trying to be clever'. The sermon - like every effort to communicate - is actually a work of art, and needs to be treated as such.

Art can be a spiritual experience for people. A poem, painting, story, film or sculpture has the power to give people a taste of what lies beyond themselves. This is one of the ways in which God has weaved revelation into the fabric of what it means to be human. The sermon is unique among art in that the explicit contract between artist and audience is that God is front and centre. Some people turn hostile if they suspect that you're trying to sneak God into areas where He's forbidden, but with the sermon you're allowed to be blunt.

Because of this, I find myself squirming in the pew if I suspect that I'm listening to a preacher who takes more care over constructing e-mails than he does over sermons.

"It's about God. It's got nothing to do with me," is an excuse used by sometimes well-meaning, sometimes lazy preachers who think that God is a KitchenAid mixer – you just throw in the ingredients, and leave Him to it. This approach denies one of the fundamental concepts of the Bible, namely that God, as an act of love, freely delegates *to us* responsibility for His reputation and message.

It's got nothing to do with human effort or creative manipulation, rather it recognises that art and communication have divinely-ordained rules. Don't tell me that Jesus, who painted pictures of plank-eyed people, camels squeezing through needles, and angry vineyard workers didn't take *how* he communicated at least as seriously as *what* he communicated.

I'm not saying that every preacher needs to be a poet, or that clever structure is an adequate substitute for a vibrant relationship with God. What I *am* saying is that every preacher needs to realise that things like language and format actually matter. A preacher doesn't need to succeed in creating art, but a preacher needs to at least *try*.

How I Put Myself Outside the Church

07 September 2017

One of the most unchristian aspects of my character is that I don't like to eat with others. If it's lunchtime, and the house is empty, I enjoy the thrill of choosing whatever food I want, taking however long I want to prepare it, and then sitting and enjoying it in the silence of a good book, or the rumblings of an even better film. I'm going to level with you; offer me the choice between a fantastic Indian meal with good friends, or a lonely peanut butter sandwich in front of the television, and it's by no means a foregone conclusion.

Those of you who felt a sympathetic shiver of approval as they read that last paragraph may be a little disconcerted to hear me describe such a thing as 'unchristian'. "The problem with you, James," you might say, "is that I can't tell when you're joking." Well, you know what? Neither can I.

I'm afraid that it's the Bible that's done it. Its pages are littered, right there in black ink, with words that tell me that great things happen when people gather together to eat.

We have no record of the amazing things that Jesus reflected on when he sat down to eat cheese and crackers by himself, but so very many stories of what happened when he sat down to eat with others. Have you ever noticed how many of Jesus' parables, teachings and miracles occurred while he was at a meal table? It's surprising. Even the risen Jesus couldn't help himself. Whether it's the fish barbecue on the beach, or the bread broken with two weary travellers on the road to Emmaus, Jesus makes himself known over food.

In Acts 2, Luke writes that one of the defining characteristics of the infant Church was that "[t]hey broke bread in their homes and ate together with glad and sincere hearts…" When Paul is writing to Corinth, instructing them on how to punish an unrepentant man who had brought public shame on the church, he says the worst thing that he can think of: "With such a man do not even eat."

How interesting it is. We live in a world obsessed with food, yet all we ever talk about is what we should eat, when we should eat and how much we should eat. We never talk about the fact that God's presence when two or three are gathered together in His name refers not just to prayer meetings, but to fish and chips too.

Acts 2:32-37 for the Modern Pulpit

14 September 2017

" **G**od has raised this Jesus to life, and we are all witnesses of the fact. 33 Exalted to the right hand of God, he has received from the Father the promised Holy Spirit and has poured out what you now see and hear. 34 For David did not ascend to heaven, and yet he said, 'The Lord said to my Lord: "Sit at my right hand 35 until I make your enemies a footstool for your feet." 36 Therefore let all Israel be assured of this: God has made this Jesus, whom you crucified, both Lord and Messiah."

32 ...

37 When the people heard this, a few said to Peter and the other apostles, "Brothers, thank you. I enjoyed that."

And a few said, "Oh, I love Psalm 110. Let me tell you what I like about it."

And a few said, "I think I've heard that sermon before."

And a few said, "That was too simple. I wish you'd go a bit deeper."

And a few said, "It wasn't as good as last week's sermon."

And a few said, "It was too short."

And a few said, "No, it was too long."

And a few said, "That was just what my friend needed to hear."

And a few were cut to the heart and thought, "Brothers, what shall we do?" but they didn't say it out loud, or to anybody else, and by the time they were sitting down to their Sunday lunch they were already thinking about what they were going to do that afternoon and didn't give Peter's words another thought.

Death by Watching

21 September 2017

Above the waist Philip oozed calm confidence, but underneath the desk his foot tapped like a woodpecker. Opposite him, the young executive leaned back in his swivel chair, Philip's CV in one hand and a twirling pen in the other.

"I see that you've got plenty of experience in television, Mr Hendrickson."

"Yes," said Philip.

Pause.

Say something else, you idiot!

"Yes," Philip repeated. "Plenty of experience."

Well, that was *fantastic*.

"It's good," the executive continued, "that you know what it takes to provide high quality amusement. That's what we need."

"'Amusement'?" said Philip.

"Sorry?" said the executive.

"You said 'amusement'? I thought this was more of a…an educational type of channel."

The executive laughed. "Entertainment is education, Mr Hendrickson."

"Of course," said Philip, blushing. Entertainment is education? What did that even mean?

"I have to say," said the executive, ignoring Philip's embarrassment, "that I'm very impressed with what I've seen today. I think you'll fit in well at Big Jesus TV. *Very* well."

Philip's nervous foot slowed to a stop.

"You're offering me the job?"

"Well," the executive placed the CV on his desk and threw Philip a winning smile, "let's just say that you can expect an encouraging phone call later today."

"Great!" Philip really meant it.

"Do you have any questions?" The executive leaned forward, elbows on the desk and hands clasped together.

"Actually, I do. You want me to work on this program, *Super Amazing Mission Stories*, about people telling others about Jesus, right?"

"Yes." The executive rested his head on his intertwined fingers and grinned.

"Well, I was wondering, where do the stories come from?"

The executive lifted himself from the desk, leaned back in his chair again and gestured vaguely.

"Here and there. Books. The Internet. We get them from all over the place really. Most of them need, you know, tweaking a bit."

"Tweaking?" said Philip.

"Yeah, to make them more…interesting. More exciting." The executive tapped the side of his nose knowingly. "So that God gets more glory, of course."

Philip waited.

"I don't understand. Are you saying that you make bits up?" he said, eventually.

"Bingo," said the executive, his finger swooping to point at Philip as though he were picking him out of a crowd.

"Is that...is that OK?" said Philip.

The executive shrugged. "Jesus made stories up all the time. It's basically the same thing."

"Oh," said Philip. He'd never thought about it like that before.

"It's our goal, to beam exciting and inspirational stories to the millions who subscribe to our service. But not too inspirational, hey?" said the executive, with a conspiratorial wink.

"But isn't that the point? To inspire others to share their faith?"

"Philip," said the executive, shaking his head, "can I call you Philip?"

"Please do."

"Philip, think about it. If people are out there," the executive said, waving his hand at the wall, "sharing their faith, what *aren't* they doing?"

"Ummmm," said Philip, "watching TV?"

"Exactly! We don't provide Big Jesus TV in order to encourage people to *not watch* Big Jesus TV. Can you imagine that? What would our advertisers say?"

The executive burst out laughing, as though he'd just heard the punchline to an exceptionally good joke.

"So you want people to be watching your channel rather than actually doing stuff for God?" said Philip.

"Watching our channel *is* doing stuff for God. When you're watching Big Jesus TV you're being edified and built up. You can't be out shoplifting or committing adultery while you're watching us, can you?"

"No, I suppose not," said Philip. He thought he was beginning to understand. "I guess that if people are going to be consumers, they should at least be consuming something worthwhile."

"I knew you'd fit in here!" The executive slammed his fist on the desk. "That's the Big Jesus mindset to a tee. Though I don't like to call people 'consumers'. It's a bit demeaning. I prefer the term 'addicts'."

"'Addicts'?"

"Yes. Consumers are wishy-washy and will head off as soon as they get the slightest sniff of a better bargain. Addicts are dependable. They'll never leave you in the lurch. Being addicted to God is good, right?"

"And being addicted to Big Jesus TV?" said Philip.

"For most people, it's the same thing," said the executive. "Trust me."

Redemption Walks Softly and Carries a Big Stick

28 September 2017

There is a big man waiting at the gate. He is carrying a huge wooden club. It has a nail in it. His name is Redemption. Do you let him in?

Blood sacrifice and murdered prophets in the Old Testament; Jesus and a persecuted church in the New. Redemption is a glorious word, a magnificent thing, but it leaves a scar. There is no redemption without a big club with a nail in it. Why would God do such a thing? Because redemption involves a tearing and a rending; it involves having the umbilical cord that ties us to this broken world surgically severed. Why would it not hurt? If you expect pain-free redemption then you haven't understood what you are being redeemed from.

Imagine this: A woman finds out that her husband is a gambling addict, and has spent the last twelve months frittering away the children's inheritance. True, she has not been a perfect wife, but she knows that she has not been a bad wife. She did not drive her husband to this; he chose the path of the spoiled brat. She is a woman more sinned against than sinning. So what does she do? She must carry his sin, and its consequences. She must explore the burden of forgiveness and all the ugly feelings that make it real.

But she has her own dark side. She struggles with the urge to keep her husband's failure a secret. She is afraid of the shame. For so long all she's wanted is the perfect family, the kind of family that arouses jealousy in the hearts of struggling parents and unhappy spouses alike. And for a while she had it. Why not? She worked hard for it. She deserves it. But if her husband's actions come out then she loses it all. So what does she do? In the midst of this hurt and pain and wrong she is forced to come face-to-face with something that she didn't realise was there. Her own pride.

It's not fair! She is the wounded party, the victim, the wronged one, so why won't God leave her alone? But the Holy Spirit, who watched her build her house on the sand, now watches – through the same tear-stained eyes – to see what she will do next. Not only does she have to deal with the fallout from her husband's actions, her own sin has been exposed. It's not the main event, sure, but it's out there now. Listen! Can you hear Redemption at the gate, dragging his club behind him? This is her chance to not only redeem her husband and their relationship, but it's also her chance to redeem herself. It's her chance to walk away from the unstable house that she has built and wander in the desert for a while, trusting in nothing but the uncertain and terrifying love of God. Now Redemption is knocking. Does she let him in?

No-one ever said that redemption was fair, but it is most definitely good.

The Big Bad Wolf

05 October 2017

Of all the temptations that men face, the temptation of power is the one that scrubs up the best. No-one can deny the lure of sex and money, but it's a lot harder to make your interest in those look noble. But power? Well, who doesn't want to change the world for the better? Who doesn't want to use their influence for good, to improve the lot of the downtrodden common man? Who doesn't secretly believe that although power corrupts, it won't corrupt me?

I don't know if it was what Tolkien intended, but his One Ring is a fine metaphor of what power can do to us. No matter how well-intentioned, how noble the goal, taking hold of the One Ring is to invite corruption. Handling power wisely requires a certain strength of character. I've already quoted Martyn Lloyd-Jones in a previous blog, but his insightful comment bears repeating: "The worst thing that can happen to a man is for him to succeed before he is ready."

Power gives you influence over other bearers of God's image. This is a delicate and weighty responsibility. If you wield power then your feet should permanently be bare, for you are always on holy ground. Love is patient, love is kind. It is not proud, it is not self-seeking. Love always protects.

Why do you think that the meek will be the ones to inherit the earth? Who else would God trust with it?

My Family and Other Disorders

12 October 2017

In this past week our son Parker has been diagnosed with Asperger's, except it's not called Asperger's any more. It's called Autistic Spectrum Disorder (ASD), except it won't be called that for long. They're changing it to Autistic Spectrum Condition (ASC) because, I assume, that Conditions are less offensive than Disorders. This diagnosis is not bad news for us. We'd assumed that he was autistic for a while now, and had been treating him appropriately. I imagine we're not alone in being parents who were very relieved to hear that he has ASD, rather than the alternative ("We're sorry Mr & Mrs Webb. He's not autistic, he's just really obnoxious.").

It's business as usual for the Webb family really, except that now we have access to various resources and courses that will help us be better parents for him and for his siblings, who struggle more than we do with managing their frustration at his seemingly irrational way of approaching life.

The reality is that no children are easy to raise, and each one should be treated uniquely anyway. In that regard, Parker is just like the rest of them. As difficult as it can be, I enjoy the variety I find in my own house – most of the time, anyway. Our home is a glorious circus; I alternate between being paralysed by laughter and grinding my teeth down to their stumps. I think that family life, like being part of any community, is one of God's ways of giving us an insight into what it's like for Him. Would Adam and Eve have been in such a rush to become like God if they had really known that it was less about exercising unlimited power and more about repeatedly having to tidy up after other people who act like you don't exist?

Raising a child with ASD is a challenge, and it brings into the light all those failings that your other children didn't manage to expose, but I think about the patient, generous way that God has raised me, and it helps.

An Opportunity to Reflect

19 October 2017

When I was training to be a minister they made me do something that they called 'theological reflection'. Each week I had to choose an experience I'd had in the last seven days and write a short reflection on it. I had to ponder over what had happened, how I'd responded, whether I'd do anything different and so on. Part of this process involved thinking through what the event and my responses revealed about God, the Bible, human nature and the like. I didn't look forward to this enforced weekly introspection. It's an odd way to live, having something major happen in your life and be thinking, "Oh good! I'll have something to write about this week." But, like many unpleasant disciplines, it achieved its purpose. After a couple of years, the habit became ingrained. Now I couldn't stop theologically reflecting on stuff even if I wanted to.

After a few years of living in Australia, I returned briefly to the UK for a winter pilgrimage of sorts. I did a whistle-stop tour of most of the places that I had lived, or had been significant in some way, and took the time to stop, listen and reflect. At each location I asked myself a question: "What did I learn about God while I was here, and how did I experience Him during this stage of my life?" It was an excellent use of a plane ticket.

I'm telling you this because I am an advocate for reflection, in whatever form it takes. Reflect on your day-to-day life; reflect on significant, epoch-shaking moments; reflect on how you live and what it says about your faith; reflect, and make a habit of reflecting. 'The unexamined life is not worth living', and all that jazz.

And a final word to a few of you – you will know who you are. After 27 years, the Canowindra campus of Cornerstone is closing down. On the 18th November the community there is setting apart some time to share stories, reflect and say goodbye. If you had a significant experience at Canowindra, and if you're able to go, then take advantage of the opportunity. It can be hard to grab time for pilgrimage and reflection, but it's good for you.

What Hosea Said

26 October 2017

Here's a twelve year old sermon that I've edited into a blog post. This one was on Hosea 6 & 7, and is a bit longer than the last sermon I revisited on these pages. It also required a lot more editing — I had to remove some especially dated references. Listen, it's not that I'm too lazy to come up with something original — it's rather that I don't think I'll ever preach this sermon again, so I'm putting it on the internet for posterity. Yes, that's it.

I have a friend. Some of you will have a friend like this. He keeps making harmful decisions, because he's…well, I don't know why he does it. It's not as bad now, thankfully, but back when we hung out it was crazy. It would be easier to understand if he wasn't a Christian, but he is. He's been a Christian since he was young, but he walks this fine line with his faith. It's not that he's not committed, or not sincere. To be honest, I just don't know what it is.

He goes through up and downs, like most of us. Sometimes he's passionate about God, sometimes he's not. He knows his Bible. He knows it well, and he's got a good grasp of theology.

But, well, it's almost like he knows it, but he never lets the information make the journey from his head to his heart. It's like he's going through the motions a lot of the time, because he knows it's what he should be doing, and thinking, and feeling, but it's as though it's not quite real for him. But again, he's sincere. He knows who Jesus is, but he just doesn't seem to be able to make the connection between that and living for God.

Take relationships, for example. He just makes bad choices when it comes to women. It's not even that he goes out with non-Christians. He meets girls at church that are just as messed up as he is. In the two year period that I was closest to him, he had four girlfriends and none of them were good for him. It's like these relationships seem to shut God out of his life. They never last, but I reckon that's a good thing, because as damaging as these relationships are in the short term, I dread to think what he'd be like if he'd been going out with one of these girls for years rather than months.

He's highly suggestible too. Easily swayed by outward appearances and advertising. Suckered in by any and every half-baked scheme, wasting his money on stuff that can't help him. He knows that Christ alone offers satisfaction and health; he knows this. But like I said, he doesn't *know* it. He was always showing me the stuff he'd bought. He was always showing me and telling me about his new toy and how it was the thing that he'd really been after – but he got through stuff pretty quickly. Some of my other friends did very well off him, waiting for him to get bored with his new purchase and then buying it from him on the cheap.

I remember one conversation we had outside Currys. We were waiting for a bus and he was talking to me about Jesus and God and stuff. He was saying all the right things, about how he'd just got out of one of those destructive relationships. He was telling me how he'd really drawn strength from his faith, and how he felt closer to God, and that he realised that God was all that he needed and the source of the hope that he'd been missing. He said that he needed to get that relationship back on track. But it was weird; he was saying all this, and I noticed that as he was talking his eyes were drifting, until it was obvious that he was looking elsewhere.

I followed his gaze to see that he was looking in the shop window, at a huge widescreen TV. There was no sound, but it was the adverts. He was there talking to me about God, but watching the adverts. That kind of sums him up really. Talks the talk, says the right things, and knows the right things, but is focused on something else. His mind is elsewhere. Talks about God, but watches the adverts.

It wouldn't be so bad, but he really didn't have a clue what he was like. He just didn't get it. He knew something was wrong, but he didn't understand what. He didn't know that he was doing it to himself. I tried to tell him. Lots of people tried to tell him. I'm not the only one. He's been very blessed, really, that God has sent a constant stream of people to try and show him and tell him that something's got to change, but he never really makes the connection. Sometimes he gets close. Sometimes he says something that makes you think, "Wow, it's finally sunk in," but soon you realise that it was a moment of clarity and nothing else. Just part of the right language he knows, but isn't sure what to do with.

Do you want to know his name? You might already know his name.

He goes by many names, but most of the time he's simply called Israel. Sometimes Ephraim. Sometimes Judah. It's all similar you know. One of his friends, a guy called Hosea, tried to make him see sense. Like I said, just one of many friends who say the same things, and it seems like he never listens.

Hosea said to him, "You've had four girlfriends in the past two years…" well, what Hosea actually said was, "You've had four kings in the past twenty years…" but it's the same thing really. Hosea said, or rather God said through Hosea, "You've had four kings in the past twenty years – and each one of them was assassinated. You know what? Not one of them ever called out to me."

What do you expect for Israel when he's in those kind of relationships? And God said to him, "It's not your ideas that are half-baked – it's you! You're like a half-baked cake. Mixed in with all the wrong ingredients and the final act, the act of turning back to Me, left undone."

God said to him, "You invest your time and money and energy into these foreign powers, these idols, and they're just robbing you. You're paying tribute to foreign powers and smiling, unaware that you're just draining yourself of your resources for no gain."

God said to him, "You're like a bird that's easily scared from branch to branch, flitting and flying here and there. Stupid, easily trapped and ensnared in something that's no good for you."

God said to him, "The worst thing is that you smile about it. You are totally unaware of what's happening. You think that this is how it should be, how I want it to be! You just don't seem to want to understand! Wake up and smell the coffee!"

That's what Hosea used to tell him. He was much better at speaking to Israel than me.

Anyway, we drifted apart. I wasn't too worried because, despite everything, he seemed to be one of those people that God had taken a special interest in, and seemed to be making a lot of effort for. I totally lost contact with him until very recently, when I bumped into him on a train – one of those chance encounters, you know. He looked really well. I didn't recognise him at first. He spotted me. I said, "You look good." He said, "Yeah, things are going well. I've changed a lot since you saw me last. Me and God, we've moved on to a new stage in our relationship. It's great. It's working very well." He did seem to be different, in a good way, but I was a little concerned. I saw it in his eyes. I noticed the way his attention flicked to an attractive girl who entered the carriage and stayed just a little bit too long. I noticed that when we were waiting at a station there was a whole chunk of the conversation that he missed because he was mesmerised by an advertising billboard on the platform. On the whole he seemed much better, it's just I was a little worried that the signs were still there, that he wouldn't have to fall too far to totally slip back to where he was.

We reached his station and he got out. "Good to see you again, Israel," I said. He smiled and said, "You too, James. But my name's not Israel anymore. I changed it. My name is Church."

Church. It seemed to suit him. But, well, you know. I hope that it lasts. I'd hate for a few years down the line his new friends to be saying exactly the same kind of things that Hosea used to say. I'd hate for it to be all as it was when I knew him, and that the only thing that had changed was that people were calling him Church instead of Israel.

ABOUT THE AUTHOR

James is a writer, a father, a husband, a follower of Jesus and a lover of board games, though not necessarily in that order. Sometimes he even manages to do some of these things quite well. He's crammed quite a lot of experiences into his life so far, such as working for Tearfund; being a Baptist minister; living in Australia as part of a mission and discipleship community and watching QPR beat Oldham Athletic at Loftus Road on the 27th December 1993. It's not been all bad.

He and his family currently live in Canterbury, England.

BOOKS BY THE SAME AUTHOR

The Listening Book:
The Soul Painting & Other Stories

This is a beautiful book, in words and images, and will appeal to old and young and all those in between. As the title suggests, the stories are perfect for reading aloud and could be used in a range of settings. The delicate images add another dimension. From fables to folk tales, from stories told around the camp fire to John Lewis Christmas ads, humankind responds to the power of story and to the meaning that narratives give us.

Sophie Duffy
Author of *Bright Stars*, *The Generation Game* and *This Holey Life*.

Job 28 pictures the search for wisdom as digging for gold. The Listening Book has numerous nuggets to mine, embedded in stories that will help you to remember them.

Steve Divall
Senior Pastor, St Helen's Church, North Kensington.

Hardback ISBN: 978-0-9934383-0-1   Softback ISBN: 978-0-9934383-2-5
EBook ISBN: 978-0-9934383-1-8 Audiobook via Amazon/Audible
Religion: Inspirational
Lioness Writing Ltd Release date: 31 October 2015
144 pages, 8.5 inches x 8.5 inches, 25 colour photographs and 3 B&W photos

The Second Listening Book:
Loaded Question & Other Stories

I enjoy reading James Webb, not just because he is a gifted and imaginative storyteller, but because he provides nourishing soul food for the journeys we all make through the deserts of life. With his creative imagination he provokes a range of emotions in the reader and I invite you to step inside and be prepared to find something for which your soul has cried out.

David Coffey OBE
Global Ambassador for BMS World Mission.

There are very few books I read that can make me laugh and think profoundly at the same time. This book however is one of them. As a child I used to watch Tales of the Unexpected and loved the twists at the end - James' book easily surpasses them. It is very easy to read and yet worthwhile at the same time as each story contains spiritual truths (which aren't at all preachy and sometimes not obvious!). This is a book you have to try - you won't regret it.

Eric Harmer
Pastor of Barton Church, Canterbury and Author of
Build-Your-Own Bible Study.

Hardback ISBN: 978-0-9934383-6-3   Softback ISBN: 978-0-9934383-4-9
EBook ISBN: 978-0-9934383-7-0 Audiobook via Amazon/Audible
Religion: Inspirational
Lioness Writing Ltd Release date: 31 October 2016
158 pages, 8.5 inches x 8.5 inches, 31 black & white illustrations and photos

The Ramblings of the Man who Bought a Pear

James's Blog started in October 2015 and has become a weekly phenomenon that adds salt and light to the internet. This first year of posts is a rich collection of things in his head that he has been brave enough to release into the wild. 'The Man who Sold me a Pear' won the 2016 Association of Christian Writers 'Good Samaritan' short story award in partnership with Street Pastors.
www.thelisteningbook.org.uk

The Association of Christian Writers is a fellowship of writers sharing prayerful support and encouragement as well as giving professional standards of training and advice. They support Christian writers overseas, in the developing world and Eastern Europe. www.christianwriters.org.uk

Street Pastors are trained volunteers from local churches who serve their community during the small hours of the weekend. Teams of men and women patrol from 10 pm to 4 am on a Friday and Saturday night, to care for, listen to and help people who are out on the streets. Proceeds from this book will help support this work. www.streetpastors.org

Comments on 'The Man who Sold me a Pear':
Anne: I had a tear in my eye too!
Jon: Can really relate to this one. Thanks for writing it.
David: I just discovered your Blog. Love it and the honesty in sharing your life and faith. This story about buying a pear really touched me. Cheers James.

Softback £5.99/$10 ISBN: 978-0-9934383-8-7
Religion: Inspirational
Published by Lioness Writing Ltd, Member of CSPA
<lionesswritingltd@gmail.com>
Release date: 31 October 2016
170 pages
8 inches x 5 inches

MORE POSTS

www.thelisteningbook.org.uk

You can contact James at

author@thelisteningbook.org.uk